German Shepherds

by Nico Barnes

www.abdopublishing.com

Published by Abdo Kids, a division of ABDO, P.O. Box 398166, Minneapolis, Minnesota 55439.

Copyright © 2015 by Abdo Consulting Group, Inc. International copyrights reserved in all countries. No part of this book may be reproduced in any form without written permission from the publisher.

Printed in the United States of America, North Mankato, Minnesota.

052014

092014

 THIS BOOK CONTAINS RECYCLED MATERIALS

Photo Credits: Glow Images, Shutterstock, Thinkstock

Production Contributors: Teddy Borth, Jennie Forsberg, Grace Hansen

Design Contributors: Candice Keimig, Laura Rask, Dorothy Toth

Library of Congress Control Number: 2013952550

Cataloging-in-Publication Data

Barnes, Nico.

 German shepherds / Nico Barnes.

  p. cm. -- (Dogs)

ISBN 978-1-62970-030-4 (lib. bdg.)

Includes bibliographical references and index.

1. German shepherds--Juvenile literature.   I. Title.

636.737--dc23

                              2013952550

Table of Contents

German Shepherds

German shepherds are strong.

They are also very smart.

German shepherds are big dogs. They can weigh up to 90 pounds (41 kg).

German shepherds have long, **bushy** tails. They have large, upright ears.

German shepherds have thick fur. It is usually black and tan.

Hard Workers

German shepherds were **bred** to be farm dogs. This is why they are hard workers.

13

German shepherds like
to learn. Having a job
to do makes them happy.

German shepherds are often police dogs. They can be military and **rescue dogs** too.

Exercise

German shepherds like
to be active. A daily
walk or jog is important.

Family

German shepherds are happiest with their human families.

More Facts

- German shepherds were first bred in Germany in 1889. They were **bred** to watch over and herd sheep.

- German shepherds often have roles in TV and in films. This is partly because they are reliable and easy to train.

- German shepherds are considered one of the smartest breeds.

Glossary

breed – a group of animals sharing the same looks and features. Breeding is raising dogs to make offspring that act and look a specific way.

bushy – full and shaggy.

rescue dog – a dog trained to assist rescue workers.

Index

abdokids.com

Use this code to log on to abdokids.com and access crafts, games, videos and more!

Abdo Kids Code:
DGK0304